A TREE IS A HOME

For Isaac, the newest leaf on our family tree. Love from Nana. — P.H.
To my friends and family — Z.Y.

Published in Canada and the U.S. by Kids Can Press Ltd.
25 Dockside Drive, Toronto, ON M5A 0B5

Kids Can Press is a Corus Entertainment Inc. company

www.kidscanpress.com

The artwork in this book was rendered in watercolor, gouache, color pencils and Photoshop.
The text is set in Segaon.

Edited by Katie Scott
Designed by Marie Bartholomew

Printed and bound in Shenzhen, China, in 3/2021 by C & C Offset

CM 21 0 9 8 7 6 5 4 3 2 1

Library and Archives Canada Cataloguing in Publication

Title: A tree is a home / written by Pamela Hickman ; illustrated by Zafouko Yamamoto.

Names: Hickman, Pamela, author. | Yamamoto, Zafouko, illustrator.

Identifiers: Canadiana 20200366718 | ISBN 9781525302367 (hardcover)

Subjects: LCSH: Forest ecology — Juvenile literature. | LCSH: Forest animals —

Habitat — Juvenile literature. | LCSH: Trees — Ecology — Juvenile literature. |

LCSH: Seasons — Juvenile literature.

Classification: LCC QH541.5.F6 H53 2021 | DDC j577.3 — dc23

Kids Can Press gratefully acknowledges that the land on which our office is located is the traditional territory of many nations, including the Mississaugas of the Credit, the Anishnabeg, the Chippewa, the Haudenosaunee and the Wendat peoples, and is now home to many diverse First Nations, Inuit and Métis peoples.

We thank the Government of Ontario, through Ontario Creates; the Ontario Arts Council; the Canada Council for the Arts; and the Government of Canada for supporting our publishing activity.

A TREE IS A HOME

PAMELA HICKMAN

ZAFOUKO YAMAMOTO

KIDS CAN PRESS

THE big, old oak tree stands tall near the empty house. It has been growing for nearly a hundred years. Many animals have lived here. Like a house, the tree provides shelter and a place to raise a family.

SOLD

Six animals share the tree
as a home. Each lives in a
different part of the tree.

A sleepy **raccoon** peeks
out of his hole in the
tree. It used to be a
home to a woodpecker
family and is still lined
with their wood chips.

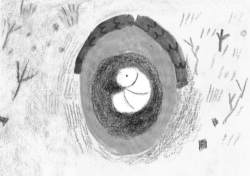

Some animals are not
so easily noticed. Hidden
inside an acorn is a tiny
acorn weevil larva.

Overnight, a young **opossum**
moved into a hollow at the base
of the tree. Like the raccoon,
she is nocturnal and prefers
to sleep during the day in her
bed of dried leaves.

In a fork near the top of the tree, a **gray squirrel** lives in her drey made of twigs and leaves.

The **blue jay** prefers to nest out in the open. He and his mate built their nest from twigs, grass, mud and roots.

A **chipmunk** burrows underground, where the tree's roots spread.

AUTUMN

Autumn brings many changes. The mornings are frosty, and the green oak leaves have turned a deep purplish red. The acorns have changed color, too, from green to brown. By late autumn, most of the leaves and acorns will have fallen off the tree and covered the ground below.

Like the tree, the animals are changing to prepare for the long winter ahead. Changes in their bodies, and to their routines and homes, will help them survive the cold.

At night, the **raccoon** eats acorns, nuts and wild grapes to gain weight — a change in his usual diet of insects, worms, fish and frogs. By late autumn, he will have a thick layer of fat for warmth. His fur grows extra thick, too, like a winter coat.

The **acorn weevil** larva chews a round hole in the side of the fallen acorn and emerges. He quickly tunnels into the soil and makes a new home where he'll be protected from the cold.

The young **opossum** leaves her new home at night to feed on birds, small mammals and nuts. Hunting more than usual will fatten her up for the coming months.

The **gray squirrel**'s fur grows thicker and longer to keep her warm. She buries hundreds of acorns below the tree to eat when fresh food becomes scarce.

The **blue jay**, too, is busy hiding acorns. He carries them in his crop, mouth and even at the tip of his beak, and hides them in the tree's bark. In the winter, he'll know where to find a meal.

The **chipmunk** gathers acorns to store in her burrow, where she will soon hibernate. She carries them underground in her large cheek pouches.

WINTER

Winter has arrived with its cold wind and snow. The oak tree survives the harsh weather by becoming dormant, or inactive. Its trunk and branches stop growing, and the dark, scaly bark acts as insulation. In the winter, the tree's sap contains more sugar to stop the tree from freezing solid and prevent damage. Inside the buds, next season's leaves and flowers are protected.

The animals are surviving the cold in many ways. Like the dormant tree, some are inactive, hibernating for most of the season. Others stay in their cozy homes only during the worst weather but still venture out for food that provides energy to keep warm. Feathers, fur and fat help insulate their bodies.

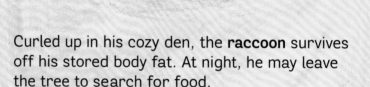

Curled up in his cozy den, the **raccoon** survives off his stored body fat. At night, he may leave the tree to search for food.

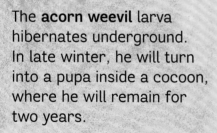

The **acorn weevil** larva hibernates underground. In late winter, he will turn into a pupa inside a cocoon, where he will remain for two years.

Her new layer of body fat helps the **opossum** stay warm, but she is not well adapted for the season. She must stay inside to survive the coldest nights. She sleeps longer than usual but does not hibernate.

During a snowstorm, the **gray squirrel** shelters in her drey. Her thick fur and bushy tail act as a blanket for extra warmth. Later, when she is out gathering food, she will find a mate nearby.

The **blue jay** stays warm by puffing up his feathers to trap air. The air acts like insulation to keep in his body heat.

The **chipmunk** hibernates inside her underground burrow. To save energy, her body temperature lowers and her heartbeat and breathing slow down. She wakes up every few days to eat the acorns she gathered in autumn.

SPRING

Spring is a time of new life. The oak tree's buds swell and burst, revealing green leaves. Its flowers appear at the same time. Yellowish-green male flowers, called catkins, hang down from the branches. Much smaller, reddish-green female flowers appear on new growth. Once fertilized, they will produce acorns.

In early spring, the **raccoon** leaves his den at night to look for a mate.

A different adult **acorn weevil** emerges from his cocoon after spending two years underground.

The **opossum** has given birth to eight joeys the size of honeybees. The babies climb into her fur-lined pouch, where they will feed and grow.

Like the tree, the animal families are blossoming. Many of the females give birth in the spring, when the weather is warmer and more food is available for the young. Others are just starting to look for a mate or are entering a new stage of their life cycle.

The **gray squirrel** nurses her six-week-old kits. The three babies have grown fur and can now open their eyes.

The **blue jay** feeds his mate as she incubates, or sits on, her five blue, spotted eggs. He mainly brings her insects, such as beetles and caterpillars, to eat.

The **chipmunk** snuggles in her burrow with her five pink, hairless pups. She has lined their home with extra leaves and grass to keep them warm.

SUMMER

The tree grows all summer. Its trunk grows wider and branches grow longer. Underground, the roots grow longer, too. They absorb nutrients and water from the soil to help the tree grow. The flowers have fallen off. On the twigs are large green leaves and new buds that contain next year's leaves and flowers. Green acorns, too, grow and ripen.

The **raccoon** has fathered four cubs but continues to live alone in the tree and does not help raise them. Nearby, the mother raccoon teaches the cubs to climb a tree.

The **acorn weevil** mates, and the female lays an egg inside an acorn on the tree. Soon, a tiny larva will hatch. It will grow inside the acorn, and feed on it, all summer long.

Once the babies grow too big for her pouch, the mother **opossum** carries the joeys on her back. At night, they search for fruit, seeds, insects and earthworms to eat.

Like the tree, the young animals are growing. Their parents feed and protect them, but the young are learning to find food and watch for danger as they explore their surroundings.
By the end of summer, it is time for them to leave home and begin life on their own.

The mother **squirrel** watches as her kits find berries, fruits and fungi to eat. She will be alone soon, once they seek out new homes of their own.

The **blue jay** keeps a close watch on his young. At three weeks old, they are fledglings who are learning to fly and leaving the nest.

The **chipmunk** teaches her pups to explore for food and listen for danger. They will stay together for the summer, and then the young will leave to dig their own burrows.

A year has passed, and the tree's leaves turn color once more. New acorns drop, and animals gather them for winter. Their young have grown and left. But next year, the tree will be a home to new babies again.

Many different animals will share the tree over its lifetime. Their survival will depend on it.

LIFE CYCLE OF AN OAK TREE

Pollination

In spring, wind blows pollen from an oak tree's catkin, or male flower, to a female flower on the same tree. The pollen fertilizes the female flower, and an acorn forms.

Germination

If an animal carries the acorn away from the shade of the big tree, the acorn will germinate, or sprout, after a few weeks. It sends down a root into the soil and sends up a shoot that will produce the first leaves. The sapling, or young tree, stops growing in winter. Its bark helps insulate it from the cold. Tiny buds protect next season's leaves.

Growth
The sapling begins to grow again in spring. After 20 or more years, it will be a fully mature oak tree and will start to produce its own acorns to complete the life cycle. Oak trees live 200 to 300 years on average.

LIFE CYCLES OF THE ANIMALS IN THIS BOOK

RACCOON

Raccoons mate in early spring.

About eight weeks later, the female gives birth to three to seven cubs that have light gray fur. Their eyes are closed and they don't have teeth. The mother raises them on her own.

The cubs' black masks and ringed tails appear within 10 days.

After eight weeks, the babies venture out of the den with their mother.

In summer, the mother teaches her young to hunt, climb and swim. They will stay together until the following spring. Adult raccoons live three to five years.

ACORN WEEVIL

A female acorn weevil emerges from underground in the spring and mates with a male.

She uses her long snout to make a hole in several acorns, then lays an egg inside each one.

After two weeks, a tiny white larva hatches from its egg. It spends the rest of the summer feeding on the inside of the acorn.

In autumn, when the acorn falls to the ground, the larva chews a tiny round escape hole. It crawls out and tunnels into the soil.

The weevil turns into a pupa and stays underground for up to two years, until it becomes an adult and emerges. It will live until the following winter.

OPOSSUM

Adult opossums mate in the spring, and the female gives birth to an average of eight joeys about two weeks later.

The tiny joeys crawl up their mother's belly and into her fur-lined pouch, where they each attach to a nipple.

The joeys feed and grow inside their mother's pouch for 10 weeks.

By the end of summer, the opossums are big enough for the mother to carry on her back. She teaches them to hunt for food.

In autumn, the grown opossums leave to find their own homes. They live about two years.

GRAY SQUIRREL

Gray squirrels mate in mid to late winter.

After about six weeks, the female gives birth to an average of three kits. The newborns are furless, and their eyes and ears are sealed shut for the first five weeks.

At six to eight weeks, they are fully furred and leave the nest for short distances.

The squirrels are nearly adults at 12 weeks. They venture out to find their own homes. Adults live about six years.

BLUE JAY

Blue jays mate in early spring, after building their nest together.

The female lays four to six eggs and incubates them for about two-and-a-half weeks.

The nestlings hatch and stay warm under their mother for the first two weeks. Their eyes open and their feathers grow in. The male blue jay feeds the entire family.

At three weeks old, the chicks leave the nest for the first time but stay close by.

After eight weeks, the young birds leave to make their own homes. They live about seven years.

CHIPMUNK

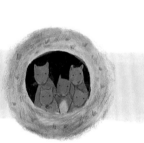

Chipmunks mate in late spring.

A month later, the female gives birth to her litter of four to six pups. The tiny babies are pink and furless. She will raise them on her own in the burrow.

After three weeks, the young chipmunks are fully furred, and a week later, their eyes and ears will open.

The young begin to leave their burrow at five to seven weeks old.

By the end of summer, the grown chipmunks leave to make their own homes. Chipmunks live two to five years.

GLOSSARY

acorn: the fruit of an oak tree

burrow: an animal's underground home

catkin: an oak tree's male flower

chick: a baby bird

cocoon: the soft, silky covering of many insects in the pupa stage

crop: a special pouch-like area in a bird's throat used to store food, such as acorns

cub: a type of young animal, such as a young raccoon

den: an animal's hidden shelter, such as a cave or tree hollow

dormant: describes a tree that is not growing but is still alive

drey: a squirrel's nest

fertilize: to combine a flower's male and female reproductive cells to form a seed

fledgling: a bird that has grown flight feathers and is learning to fly

fungi: a group of non-flowering living things, including mushrooms, molds and yeasts

germinate: to sprout and grow from a seed to a plant

hibernate: to find shelter and become inactive during the winter

incubate: to sit on eggs to keep them warm so they can develop

insulation: a substance or layer that protects from the loss of heat or cold

joey: a type of young animal, such as a young opossum

kit: a type of young animal, such as a young squirrel

larva: the pre-adult form of an insect between the egg and pupa stages

litter: two or more baby animals born together

mate (noun): the male or female of a pair of animals who produce young together

mate (verb): the union of the male and female of a species to produce young

nestling: a baby bird in a nest that cannot yet fly and is cared for by its parents

nocturnal: describes an animal that is active at night and sleeps during the day

nurse: to feed a baby milk from the mother's nipple

pollen: a powderlike substance from a flower that contains a plant's male reproductive cells

pup: a type of young animal, such as a young chipmunk

pupa: the third stage of certain insects' life cycles

sap: the sugary water that flows inside a tree

sapling: a young tree

WANT TO READ MORE?

Hickman, Pamela. *It's Moving Day!*
Toronto: Kids Can Press, 2008.

Hickman, Pamela. *Nature All Around:
Trees.* Toronto: Kids Can Press, 2019.

Karas, G. Brian. *As an Oak Tree Grows.*
New York: Nancy Paulsen Books, 2014.